Cats can't Count

WHY WE LEARN TO COUNT

BY MARIA GORDON
ILLUSTRATED BY MIKE GORDON

WAYLAND

Titles in the series:
Dogs can't Read
Mice can't Write
Cats can't Count
Spiders can't Spell

Series editor: Sarah Doughty
Book editor: Liz Harman
Cover design: Giles Wheeler/Malcolm Walker
Inside design: Malcolm Walker
Consultant: Roy Blatchford

First published in 1999 by Wayland Publishers Ltd
61 Western Road, Hove, East Sussex, BN3 1JD, England

British Library Cataloguing in Publication Data
Gordon, Maria
Cats can't count: why we learn to count. – (Animals can't)
1. Counting – Juvenile literature
I. Title
513.2'11

ISBN 0 7502 2480 0
Printed and bound by Edições ASA, Portugal

find Wayland on the Internet at http://www.wayland.co.uk

Author's thanks
The author would like to thank the many bookstore staff, teachers and librarians who gave their valuable assistance. For their generous help and support, Claire Bellanca, Ellen Kindl, and Jim Kornell are warmly appreciated, and Liz Harman deserves a medal in gratitude for all her unstinting effort, time and dedication as editor of the books in this series.

This is Kim.
Her cat is called Kit.

Kim can count.
Kit cannot.

Kim has lost a sock.
Kit has lost her kitten!

Kim can count the drawers.
Kit cannot.

Kim can find her sock.

Kit can't find her kitten.

Kim spills some
cat treats.

Kim can count the treats.
Kit cannot.

Kim finds all the treats.

Kit looks for more.

Kim wants to sit on
a bench.

Kim counts the legs
on each bench.
Kit cannot.

Kim sits down.

Kit falls off!

Kim is playing.
Kim can count the balls.

Kit can't count
the butterflies.

Kim finds all the balls.

Kit doesn't find all the butterflies.

Kim finds a tortoise.

Kim knows the number
on its shell.
Kit does not.

Kim works out where
the tortoise lives.

Kit can't
work it out.

Kim walks past
the dogs.

Kim can count the
dog dishes.
Kit cannot.

14

Kim knows there are more dogs.

Kit gets a shock!

Kim counts out
the drinks for her
friends.

Kit can't count
treats for
her kittens.

Kim's friends are happy.

Not all
Kit's kittens
are happy.

Kim is given time to tidy up.

Kim can count
the minutes.
Kit cannot.

Kim is not in trouble.

Kit **is** in trouble!

Kim's team lines up.
Kim can count the team.

Some birds aren't home.
Kit can't count them.

Kim waits for the rest
of the team.

Kit doesn't
wait for the birds.
She jumps too soon!

Kim's team scores a goal.
Kim can count the goals.

Kit can't count
the snacks.

Kim's team needs
more goals.

Kit has far too
many snacks!

Kim counts orange slices in twos for her players.

Kit sees the players' legs. She can't count in twos.

Each player gets two slices.

Kit gets dizzy!

Kim piles up the coins.
Kit spills the money!

Kim can count money.
Kit cannot.

Kim makes new piles.

Kit doesn't care!

Kim's team wins the game.

Kim can count '5, 4, 3, 2, 1, cheese!'
Kit cannot.

Kim gives three cheers.

Kit gives six!

Notes for Adults

Counting is part of general numeracy. Reinforced by imaginative play, and directed towards particular tasks, counting can quickly become a useful tool for children.

Blocks, puzzles, construction kits, even sand and water give children practical mathematical experience. Physical games with beanbags, skittles, hoops, along with finger games, number rhymes and play shops all encourage a child to think and work with numbers. It is important not to forget, though, that daily life offers many opportunities for a child to engage in counting and the mathematical thinking behind it.

The events of this book, and of any child's day, can be tied to standard counting tasks. Some of these tasks, linked to relevant pages, are set out below. Concentrate on easier ones first, re-reading later to introduce a little more difficulty. Ideas for ways to help a child understand and practise some of these tasks are also included. Relax, don't count the days it takes to achieve this, but be ready to praise when it happens!

The activities such as the 'Hunt the page number' can help children increase their familiarity with numbers, and also the search for information in books, directories or on the Internet. They also help children to learn to review material, and to practise skills basic to the use of indexes and glossaries. Such skills in turn help to enhance numeracy by increasing both awareness of its practical application and fluency.

Activities

Hunt the page number
• Use the page number hunt below to turn this book into a numeracy skills game. Ask children to search the story and illustrations to find the words and numbers in the panel below and to note the numbers of the page(s) on which they appear. Help them to put the page numbers found in order, to see which are odd and which are even, and to fill in the other numbers in the sequence.

Further skills teaching with this book:
Page 3: Join children in counting the four kittens to help them learn and recite numbers in order and back again.
• Count out loud (and silently) other items e.g. seeds for planting, money for spending etc. Show how numbers also mean cost, size, distance, time, etc. Identify numbers seen on checkout tills, appliances, etc.

game   snacks   happy

28

cheese   dizzy   fourth

bench

22

1.50

purr!   shock   money

Answers (Bold type indicates where words or numbers appear in the illustrations): bench p.8; cheese p.28/**28**; dizzy p.25; fourth p.**4** & **5**; game p.28; happy p.17; money p.26; 1.50 p.**17**; purr! p.**29**; shock p.15; snacks p.22 & 23; 28 p.**12**; 22 p.**13**.

Pages 4-5: Learn about first, second, third etc., by counting the drawers in the picture in order.
• Play simple card games and games with 'turns'. Chalk up hopscotch, hop to the fourth (second, third etc.) square, match numbered sets of keys to hooks, put away laundry and shopping, etc., identifying the second drawer, first cupboard, etc.

Pages 6/7: Help children count a set of objects, such as the cat treats. Count up how many treats have fallen on the floor. (See also pages 26-7). If Kit knew the number of treats, would she carry on looking?
• Re-count sets of items when they are rearranged e.g. chairs around the table, fish in the tank, beats of a drum etc.

Pages 8/9: Help children to take away one from a number. Using first one, then both benches, count the legs then take away the broken leg. Does Kit know how many legs there should be on a bench? What if Kit knew one bench leg was missing?
• Add one to/take away one away from a group of apples, pennies, library books, guests, phone rings. Later, add 10 to, or take 10 away from a number.

Pages 10/11: Count the footballs to show how the total of items separated into groups stays the same. Count the butterflies. Does Kit realize she's left a butterfly behind?
• Count a number of sandwiches, pennies etc., both before and after sharing them out.

Pages 12/13: Learn about counting in twos using the sequence of houses on page 13. Discuss how Kim knows quickly which house is number 28 because she counts through the sequence of numbers.
• Fill in the missing number from other two-by-two sequences. Count out items in twos from supermarket trolleys, toys from a toybox, books from a shelf. (See also pages 24-5). Later try threes, fours and fives as number sequences.

Pages 14/15: Cover over page 15, and count how many more dogs are needed to match the larger number of bowls. Would Kit be so surprised by the two extra dogs if she could compare the number of dogs to bowls?
• Find groups of different objects containing the same number of items, e.g. four oranges, four books, four crayons, etc.

Pages 16/17: Count the number of glasses on page 16 and then the number of players. How many more glasses are needed for Kim to give everyone a drink? How many more treats should Kit have brought for her kittens?
• 'Fish', in turn, with magnets for a known total of paperclips, counting how many are picked up each time. Note the different combinations of 'catches' that make up the total.

Pages 18/19: Help show addition is 'counting on' by covering over page 19 and asking the children to count on ten from the number of minutes shown on page 18. If Kit could count the minutes, would she have left the kitchen before Kit's mum returned?
• Add points to a score. Explain that this is called 'tallying'. Work out the total by counting-on.

Pages 20/21: Using Kim's team line-up, talk about numbers in sequence and missing numbers. Which missing team numbers are odd and which are even? Which of the two groups of birds is evenly numbered?
• Select teams by giving each child a number. Make one team from those with odd numbers and one from team with even numbers. Throw an even (or odd) number to start a game. Is today's date, a child's birthday, a child's age, a class number etc., odd or even?

Pages 22/23: Compare the two numbers on the score board and say which is bigger. Discuss why Kim's team needs more goals and why. How many extra sausages have been collected by Kit on page 23?
• Encourage children to keep score and count points, goals etc., during a game.

Pages 24/25: Using the full team on page 21, show how 22 slices are needed for all 11 players by counting up in twos.
• Count things that come in pairs such as shoes, socks, wheels and so on. Estimate, then confirm, how many orange slices on a plate, raisins in a mini-box, beads on a necklace, minutes before bedtime, etc.

Page 26/27: Talk about whether the amount of money will change as Kim picks up the coins and makes different piles with them.
• How many ways can a collection of money be counted?

Page 28/29: Ask who can count backwards. Talk about the numbers we enjoy and celebrate.
• Use numbers in everyday activities e.g. counting down to starting the car, talk about winning scores, anniversaries, measurements, lucky numbers, tallest buildings, biggest dinosaurs, etc. Play bingo, hold birthday parties!

Pages 6/7, 8/9, 10/11, 14/15, 18/19, 20/21, 24/25 26/27, 28/29:
Ask children to find and note down the page numbers where one kitten comes close to losing one of his nine lives in the illustrations.

Recommended reading

A Good Place for Kittens by Diane Kimpton (Scholastic, 1998)
A mother cat looks for a safe place for her kittens on a cold, rainy night. Strong, rhythmic text and evocative illustrations captures the sense of urgency of her task.

Bunny Money by Rosemary Wells (Doubleday, 1998, Picture Corgi, 1999)
Highly enjoyable, quirky story of rabbits, Max and Ruby, as Max buys presents for his grandma using his limited funds.

Each Orange has 8 Slices by Paul Giganti (William Morrow & Co., 1992/1994)
Bold simple graphics introduce counting, groups and number combinations.

One Teddy, Lots of Teddies by Debbie Mackimnon (Francis Lincoln, 1999)
Count the objects, name the colours, look for opposites and spot different shapes and sizes.

Out for the Count by Kathyrn Cave and Chris Riddel (Frances Lincoln, 1999)
When Tom finds it hard to sleep, he starts counting sheep, then pythons, pirates, tigers, goats and ghosts, counting to 100.

Over on the Farm by Christopher Gunson (Picture Corgi, 1996)
A counting picture book rhyme. Stretch with one cat, leap with two sheep or splash with three little frogs as you count from one to ten with this bouncy picture book.

Ten Black Dots by Donald Crews (William Morrow & Co., 1994)
A rhyming story for younger children which reinforces basic counting, group and number recognition. Black dots play a key role in simple illustrations of forms in the environment such as the two eyes of a fox.

Ten Cats have Hats by Jean Marzollo (Little Hippo, 1997)
Picture book about counting ducks with trucks, trees with bees and snails with trails – up to ten but keep your hat on!

Resources for adults

Curriculum Bank: Number by Cathy Hall and Lynette Kelly (Scholastic, 1995)

Useful addresses

The Basic Skills Agency is an excellent source of support material for parents and teachers involved in teaching reading, writing and arithmetic. They can be contacted at:

Commonwealth House, 1–19 New Oxford Street, London WC1A 1NU
Tel: 0207 405 4017 Fax: 0207 440 6626

Reading Is Fundamental, UK is a charitable organization that helps children grow up with a love of books and reading. It gives practical help to parents in becoming involved with their children's reading. They can be contacted at:

The National Literacy Trust, Swire House, London SW1E 6AJ
Tel: 0207 828 2435 Fax: 0207 931 9986

Book Trust is a charity which promotes the book, and manages the books for babies project known as Bookstart. They can be contacted at:

Book House, 45 East Hill, Wandsworth, London SW18 2QZ
Tel: 0208 516 2977 Fax: 0208 516 2978